SCIENCE MASTERS

WEATHER PREDICTION

Clara MacCarald

Rourke Educational Media
A Division of Carson Dellosa Education

rourkeeducationalmedia.com

ROURKE'S **SCHOOL to HOME** CONNECTIONS

BEFORE AND DURING READING ACTIVITIES

Before Reading: *Building Background Knowledge and Vocabulary*

Building background knowledge can help children process new information and build upon what they already know. Before reading a book, it is important to tap into what children already know about the topic. This will help them develop their vocabulary and increase their reading comprehension.

Questions and Activities to Build Background Knowledge:

1. Look at the front cover of the book and read the title. What do you think this book will be about?
2. What do you already know about this topic?
3. Take a book walk and skim the pages. Look at the table of contents, photographs, captions, and bold words. Did these text features give you any information or predictions about what you will read in this book?

Vocabulary: *Vocabulary Is Key to Reading Comprehension*

Use the following directions to prompt a conversation about each word.

- Read the vocabulary words.
- What comes to mind when you see each word?
- What do you think each word means?

Vocabulary Words:

- *accuracy*
- *air pressure*
- *assumptions*
- *atmosphere*
- *humidity*
- *latitudes*
- *meteorologists*
- *precipitation*
- *precise*
- *probability*
- *satellites*
- *sustained*

During Reading: *Reading for Meaning and Understanding*

To achieve deep comprehension of a book, children are encouraged to use close reading strategies. During reading, it is important to have children stop and make connections. These connections result in deeper analysis and understanding of a book.

Close Reading a Text

During reading, have children stop and talk about the following:

- Any confusing parts
- Any unknown words
- Text to text, text to self, text to world connections
- The main idea in each chapter or heading

Encourage children to use context clues to determine the meaning of any unknown words. These strategies will help children learn to analyze the text more thoroughly as they read.

When you are finished reading this book, turn to the next-to-last page for **Text-Dependent Questions** and an **Extension Activity**.

TABLE OF CONTENTS

CHAPTER ONE

A GATHERING STORM

On October 22, 2012, a tropical storm formed over the warm, moist water of the Caribbean Sea. **Meteorologists** named the storm Sandy. Tropical Storm Sandy swirled in an enormous circle with winds reaching more than 39 miles (63 kilometers) per hour. Meteorologists tracked the storm using computer models to try to predict its next move. Sandy headed north toward Jamaica.

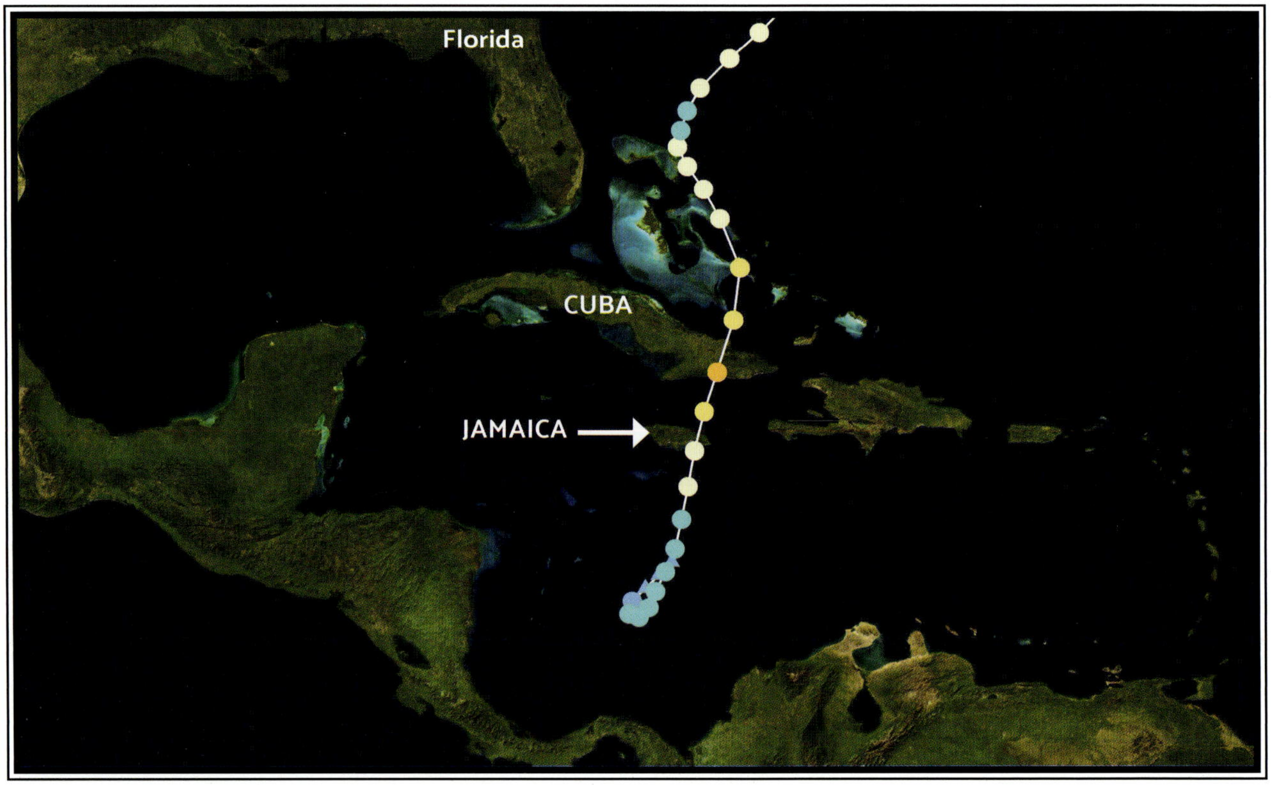

Sandy's path is shown in six-hour intervals. Following the Saffir-Simpson scale shown on page 7, the yellow and orange circles show the strongest wind speeds.

Planes can use jet streams to increase their speed.

Jet Streams

Jet streams are narrow bands of strong winds found more than 20,000 feet (6,000 meters) above Earth. They blow from west to east due to Earth's spin. Jet streams separate hot and cold air and affect how storms move. Sometimes they shift north or south, bringing unusual weather.

The storm picked up more heat and energy as it traveled, strengthening into Hurricane Sandy. Hurricane Sandy roared over Jamaica and Cuba. At its strongest, Sandy was a category three hurricane with top **sustained** wind speeds of 115 miles (185 kilometers) per hour. After leaving Cuba, Sandy's winds weakened, but its size doubled. Around that time, meteorologists noticed something strange.

In Cuba, Hurricane Sandy killed 11 people and destroyed over 15,000 homes.

There was a dome of high **air pressure** out in the Atlantic Ocean, near Greenland. The air pressure nearest the United States was low. Models predicted this would force Sandy west, toward the U.S. coast. Meteorologists alerted emergency officials, who took action to protect people in Sandy's path. The prediction proved correct several days later, when Hurricane Sandy took a sharp left turn.

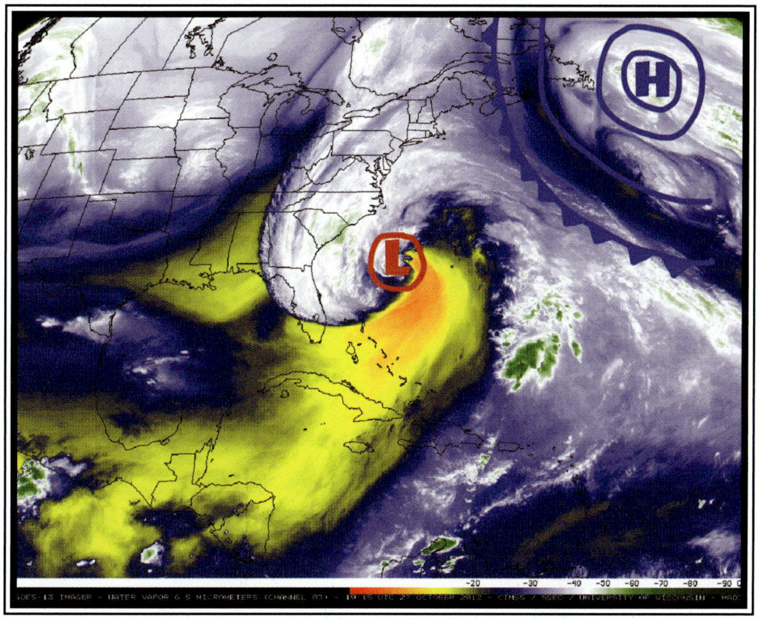

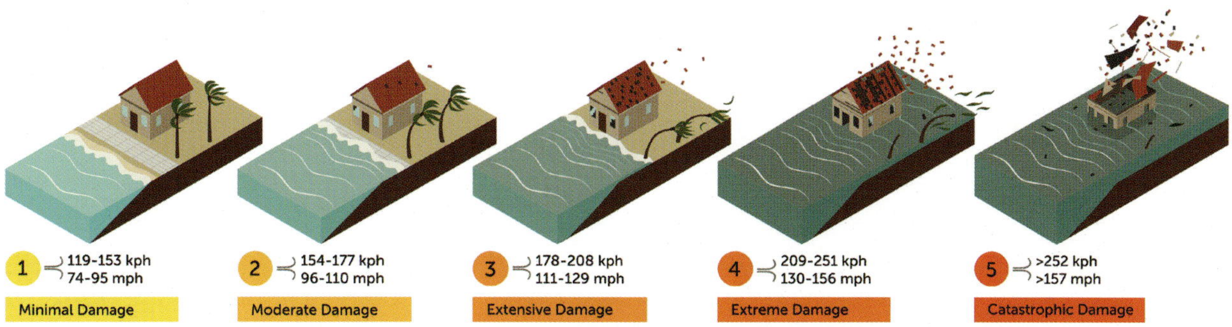

Saffir-Simpson Hurricane Wind Scale

Categorizing Hurricanes

Meteorologists sort hurricanes by their top sustained wind speeds, not by their overall size. Category one hurricanes have speeds of 74 to 95 miles (119 to 153 kilometers) per hour. Category five hurricanes, the strongest, have winds traveling 157 miles (252 kilometers) per hour or more.

Unfortunately, because the storm weakened back into a tropical storm right before it hit the U.S., some people and officials did not realize it remained very dangerous. The storm brought a surge of water from the ocean, which caused deadly flooding. When the winds cleared, Sandy had killed more than 100 people and caused damages worth billions of dollars.

Sandy brought record-setting storm surges and massive damage to some of the most populated regions of the U.S.

After Sandy, U.S. meteorologists changed how they issued warnings about storm surges. They also improved how they communicate hurricane dangers to the public. Meteorologists play an important role in society. Weather prediction helps people plan their day, helps farms and other businesses plan ahead, and can even help save lives.

Meteorologists study environmental science, math, and computer programming.

CHAPTER TWO

WHAT IS WEATHER?

The weather might seem like a simple thing. How does the air feel outside? Is the sky clear or is rain trying to wash away your front yard? Scientists define weather as the condition of the **atmosphere** over a short period of time. Weather depends on many factors such as cloud cover, wind, temperature, and air pressure.

Rainy weather can bring flooding to low-lying areas and to places where the ground cannot hold more water.

Some components of weather you can see and some you can feel. They can all be measured–if you have the right equipment in the right spot.

Temperatures near Earth's surface dip as low as -144 degrees Fahrenheit (-98 degrees Celsius) and soar as high as 159 degrees Fahrenheit (71 degrees Celsius).

Weather changes all the time. The driving force behind changes in the weather is the sun, which heats the surface of Earth unevenly. This helps create air masses. An air mass is an enormous body of air in which each part has a similar temperature, air pressure, and **humidity**. Where air masses bump up against each other, they form fronts, which often create weather events.

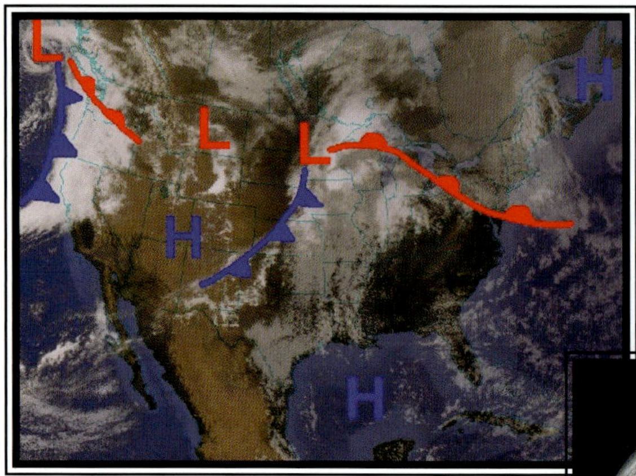

Cloud cover affects how much sunlight reaches Earth.

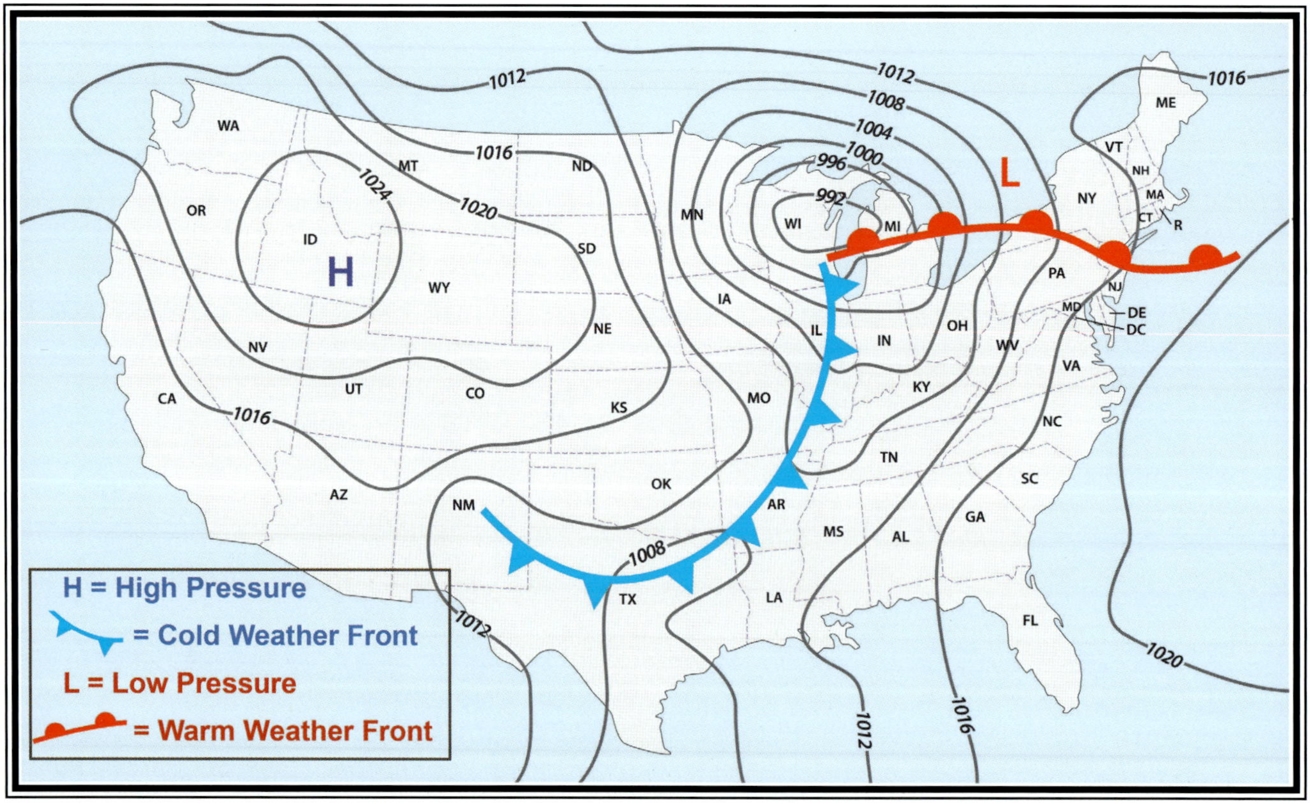

Colliding fronts create turbulence, bringing gusty winds, storms, and changes in temperature.

Climate determines what kind of weather an area tends to have.

Weather occurs over a short period of time. The weather conditions in an area over long periods of time make up its climate. Just because the weather changes, it does not mean that the climate is changing. Climate changes happen over decades and centuries. Many factors affect an area's climate.

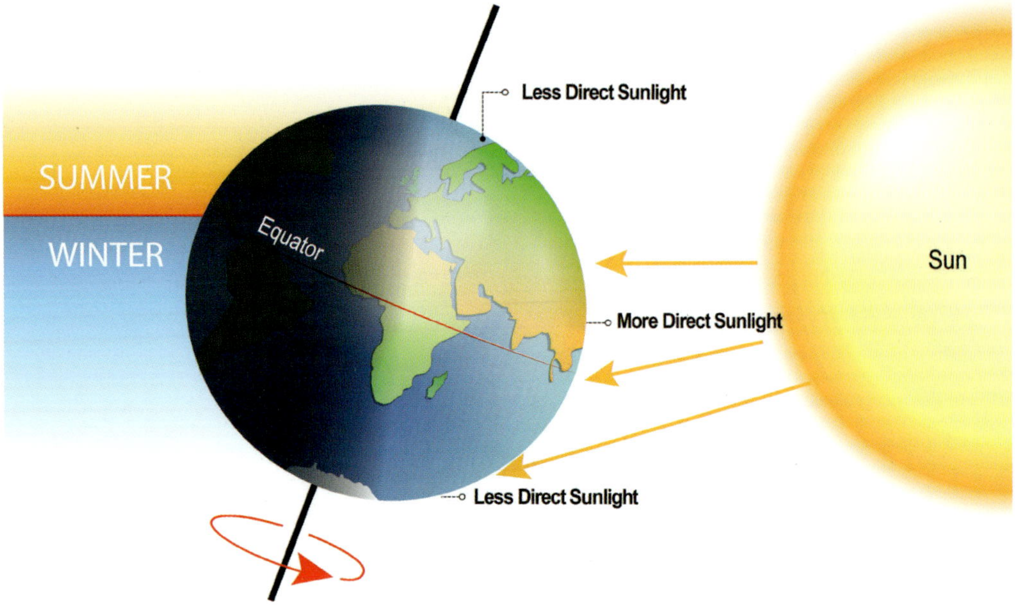

The seasons are a result of Earth's tilt, not from the planet's distance to the sun.

In general, higher **latitudes** are colder because they receive less direct sunlight. It is warmer the closer you get to the equator. However, increasing elevation also cools the air. That's why high mountains near the equator can have glaciers.

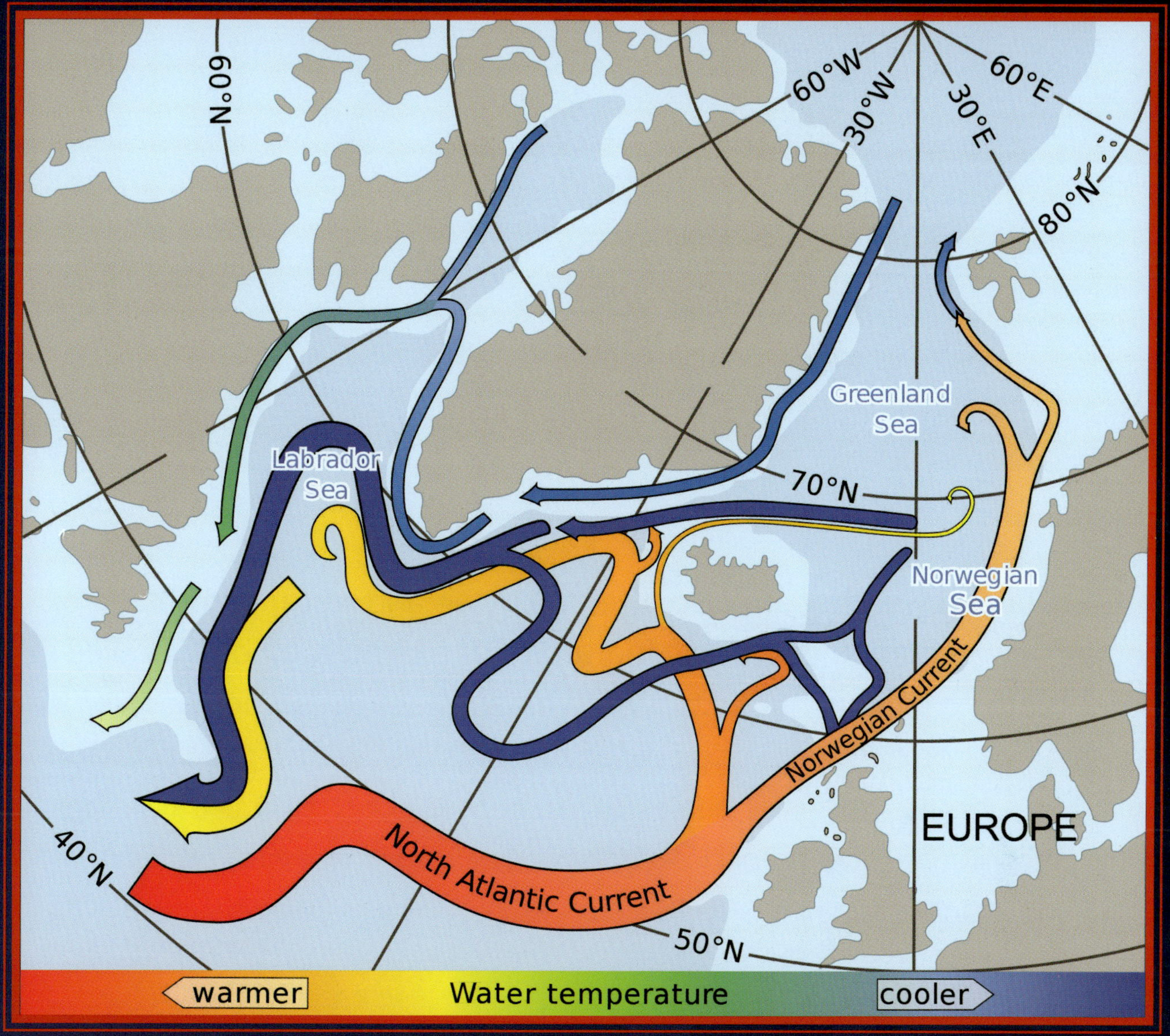

North Atlantic Current

Europe is warmer than it should be based on its latitude, and it has the Atlantic Ocean to thank. A current of warm water sweeps up the Atlantic Ocean from the south, bringing warmer weather to the continent. The current's future is uncertain, though. Researchers have seen signs of it weakening.

Air picks up moisture as it moves over bodies of water.

Climate and weather are also affected by air and water currents, bodies of water, and geographic features. For example, air over bodies of water tends to pick up humidity. When an air mass rises, such as over a mountain, it cools down. Since colder air holds less water, **precipitation** falls. The air mass brings dry air to the other side of the mountain. These kinds of patterns have helped people predict their local weather for thousands of years.

Warm air flowing over a cool body of water produces fog.

El Niño and La Niña

Climates can include year-to-year variations. For example, conditions in the Pacific Ocean affect temperature and precipitation in much of the world. When Pacific waters are unusually warm, they produce an El Niño year with warm and wet weather patterns. Cold waters produce a La Niña year with the opposite conditions.

CHAPTER THREE

A HISTORY OF PREDICTING WEATHER

In the past, farmers relied on almanacs—books that provided all sorts of information, including weather predictions for the year.

People have always watched the weather. A storm could spoil a hunt or drench people foraging for food. Sailors wanted to know what to expect on their voyages. Farmers needed to know when to plant and harvest. Ancient people kept track of the seasons and learned their local weather patterns. They looked to the sky, using clouds and wind to predict what weather might be coming.

Seafarers have an old saying about the weather: Red sky at night, sailor's delight. Red sky in morning, sailor's warning. Sometimes there is truth to this: When a high pressure air mass is to the west, the setting sun makes red colors, and good weather is probably coming.

Anvil-shaped clouds form when rising air hits a layer of warmer air. The cloud can't go any higher. Instead, the top spreads out.

Cloud Signs

Clouds are made of water. Clouds form when water droplets or ice crystals gather around particles in the atmosphere. Towering or anvil-shaped clouds often indicate a thunderstorm coming. Dark clouds tend to hold more rain than light clouds. Some clouds look threatening but form in the absence of severe weather.

Early people also took note of animal and plant behaviors. Animals can respond to subtle cues such as pressure changes that humans miss. They may act differently before a storm hits. People watched for migratory birds to arrive and plants to flower in the hopes that these signs would tell them about seasonal weather.

In the mid-1800s, people began using barometers to measure air pressure.

Punxsutawney Phil is the groundhog who appears on Groundhog Day in Pennsylvania each February. Phil is said to make a prediction. If he sees his shadow, there will be six more weeks of winter weather.

In places such as Babylonia, China, and India, ancient people recorded weather events. They created detailed systems for weather prediction. While some people thought the gods caused the weather, philosophers in Greece and Rome looked for natural causes. In the 1400s, people started developing more **precise** ways to record the weather. Over the next few centuries, inventors created instruments that measured humidity, atmospheric pressure, and temperature. They also devised units to express their measurements in.

Sending and receiving messages by telegraph was time-consuming, but it revolutionized people's ability to share information.

With all these new tools, scientists could study the causes of weather in far greater detail than ever before. In the 1800s, inventors developed the telegraph. People could use telegraphs to send and receive information about the weather all over a country. They could also send warnings of bad weather. Weather prediction began to improve by leaps and bounds.

Telegraphs could send electrical signals over a wire. Morse code assigned letters to those signals in order to send messages.

Meteorological organizations at 900 locations around the world send up weather balloons twice each day.

Measuring the Atmosphere

In the 1700s, people started using kites to measure conditions high in the atmosphere. Then came hot air balloons and helium balloons, which carried scientists and their instruments aloft. In the early 1900s, inventors created weather balloons, which were safer and could travel higher than balloons with a crew.

In 1783, two French brothers became the first humans to ride in a hot air balloon.

CHAPTER FOUR

COMPUTERS MODEL THE WEATHER

Today, people can use the internet to glance at weather predictions over an entire country before they go about their day. Where do these predictions come from? Once, meteorologists would have calculated them by hand. Now they use supercomputers. Supercomputers can work with a vast number of measurements which would overwhelm a human mind. They consider factors such as temperature, air pressure, precipitation, wind, cloud cover, and sunlight.

Smartphones can get weather forecasts from around the world in an instant.

Early computers were big and slow. In 1950, meteorologists spent over 24 hours to produce the first 24-hour computer-generated weather forecast.

Modern supercomputers make quadrillions of calculations each second. A quadrillion is a number followed by 15 zeros.

At weather stations, white colors reflect heat so that instruments don't get too hot.

To produce the data needed by supercomputers, meteorologists have electronic eyes all over the world. **Satellites**, planes, and drones spy on the atmosphere from above. They can take pictures of clouds, detect temperatures, and use Doppler radar to measure precipitation. Doppler radar systems send radio waves into the air. The waves hit objects such as raindrops and bounce back. By measuring the returning wave, the system determines the objects' size, distance, and movement.

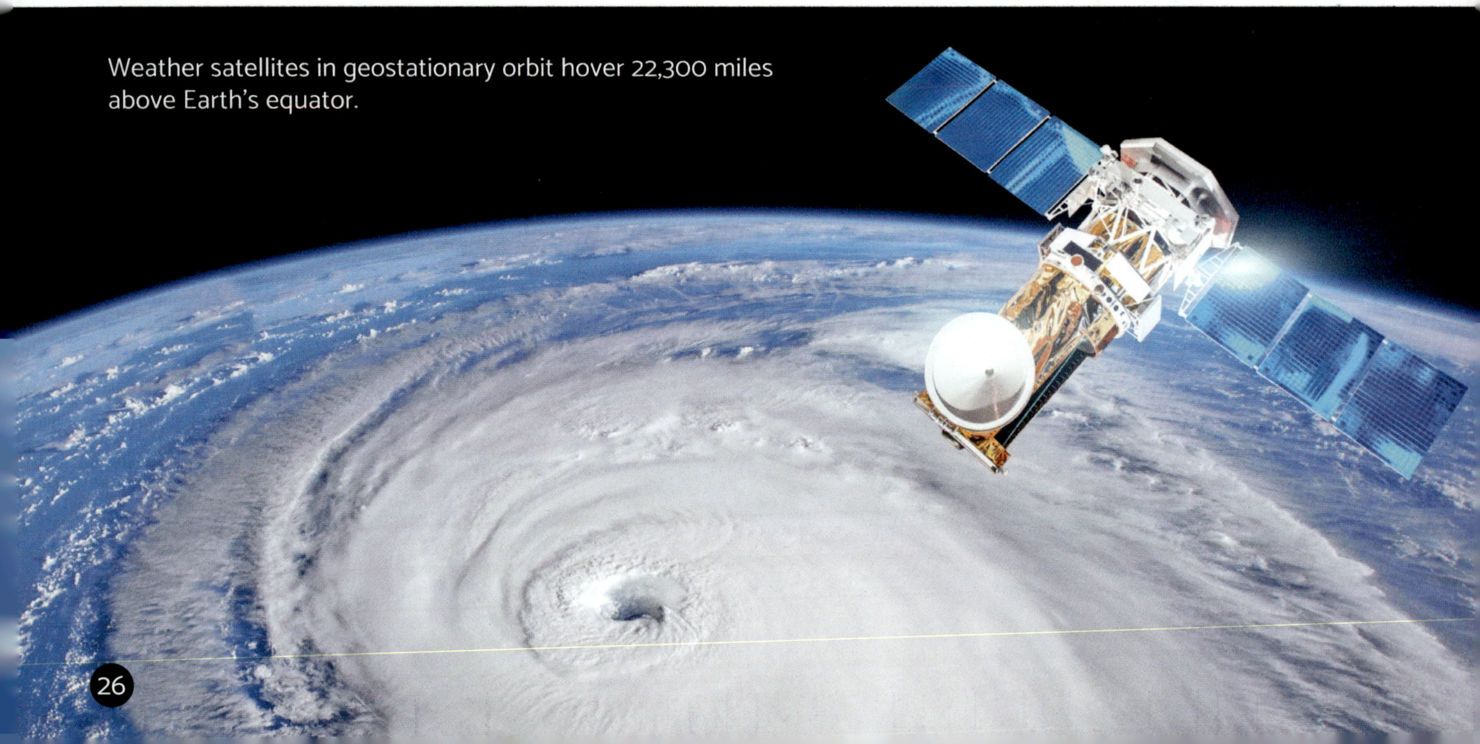

Weather satellites in geostationary orbit hover 22,300 miles above Earth's equator.

Weather balloons can measure the atmosphere directly. Radar towers detect precipitation, clouds, and wind. Weather stations and buoys record conditions at the ground or on the water.

Some weather buoys stay anchored to the sea floor. Others collect data as they drift along the waves.

Supercomputers take the data and feed it into models. Computer models are pretend versions of the real world. They include geographic features. They also use certain **assumptions** about how specific conditions affect the changing weather. Different models have different assumptions. Therefore, they usually come up with different predictions for the same situation. To deal with this, meteorologists sometimes consider several models together.

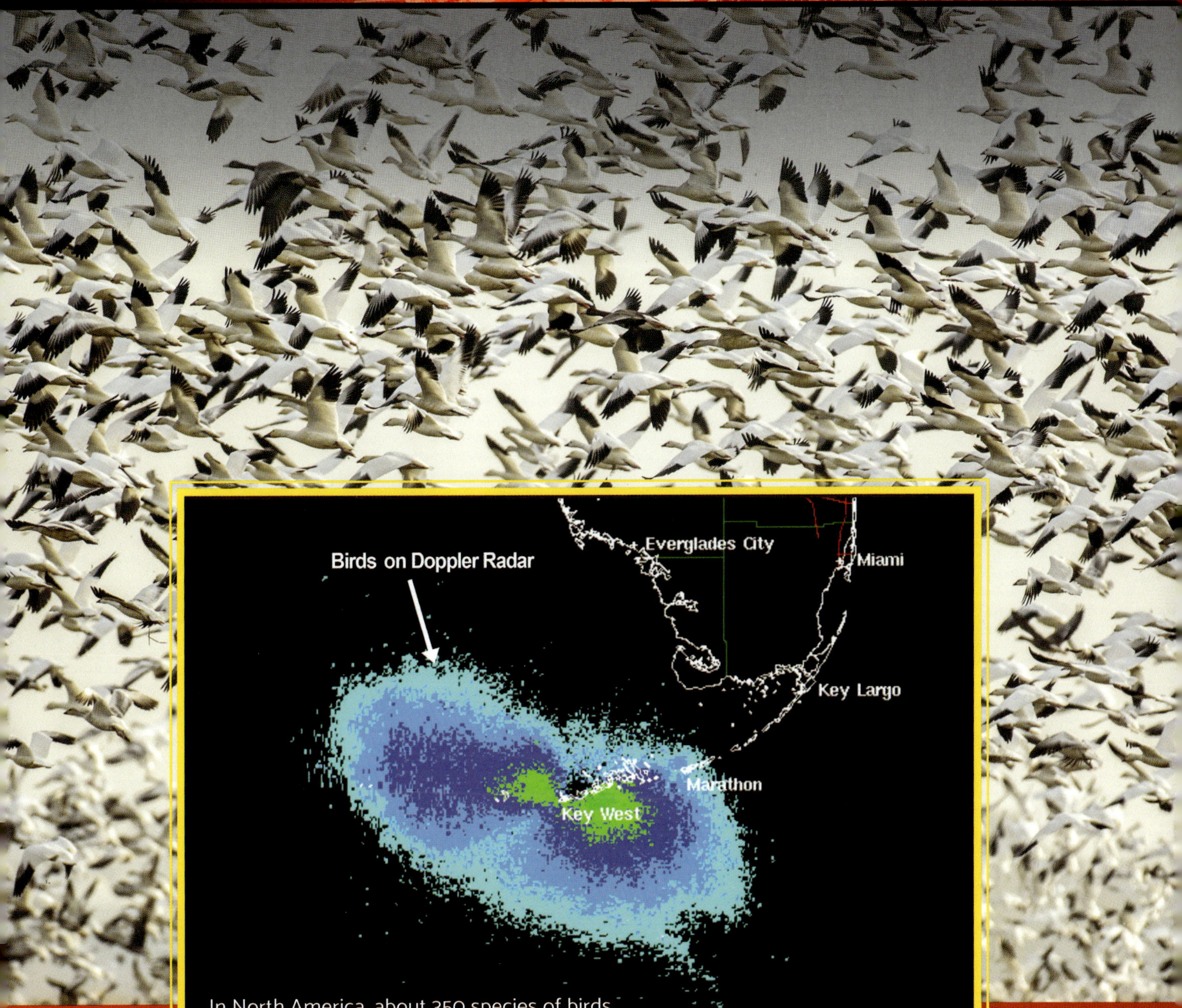

In North America, about 350 species of birds migrate thousands of miles each year.

A Cloud of Birds

Not everything in the atmosphere is part of the weather. Twice a year, huge flocks of birds migrate between their winter and summer grounds, traveling mostly at night. Bats and monarch butterflies migrate as well. These animals show up on Doppler radar just like raindrops do.

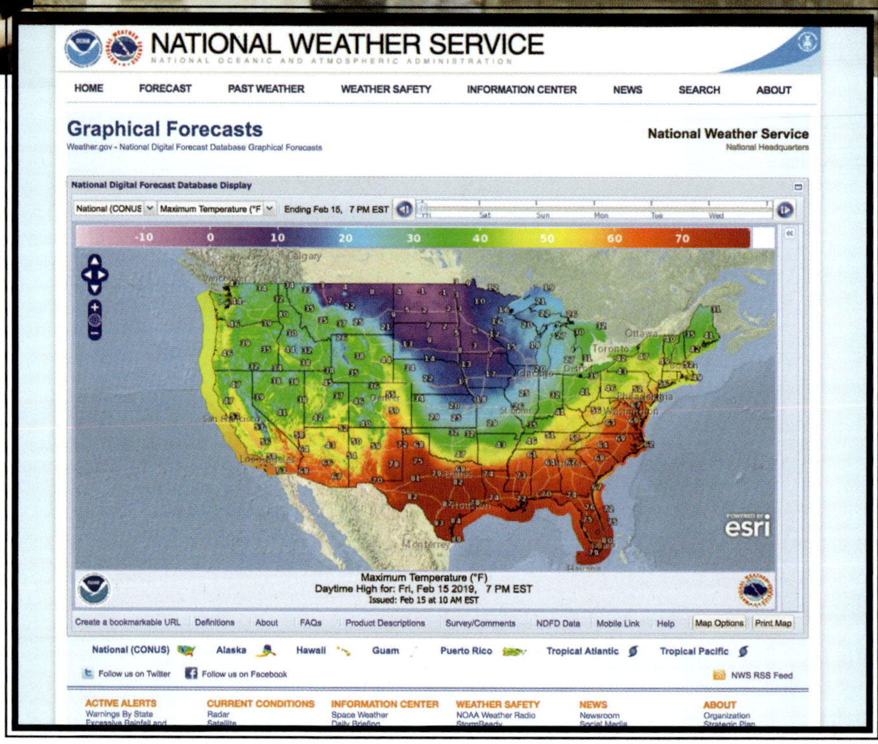

The mission of the National Weather Service (NWS) is to provide weather information to U.S. citizens for their protection and safety.

Weather predictions often include a **probability**, because no model can take into account all factors. If a model shows a 50 percent chance of rain, you can expect that it would rain half the time such conditions occurred. If rain doesn't happen, that doesn't mean the model was wrong. It only means that it was one of the times those conditions didn't lead to rain falling.

Faint lines on weather maps connect areas that have the same air pressure.

Weather Maps

Meteorologists first drew weather maps by hand in the 1800s, but now they create them with computers. A blue line with triangles means a cold front. A red line with bumps shows a warm front. Words or symbols indicate weather events. The maps may also show temperature or air pressure.

CHAPTER FIVE

STORMY SKIES

Predicting severe weather is serious business. Every year in the United States alone, weather and climate events cause about 650 deaths and about 15 billion dollars in damage to property.

Whether to expect sunshine or clouds makes a difference to someone planning a day at the beach. But knowing when a blizzard will hit, or whether conditions are right for tornadoes, can help save lives.

Tornadoes kill around 70 Americans every year.

In the U.S., tornadoes strike most often in "Tornado Alley," a region that includes Texas, Oklahoma, Kansas, and Missouri.

Severe weather includes hurricanes, thunderstorms, tornadoes, blizzards, drought, strong winds, and hail. Heavy precipitation or snowmelt can cause deadly flooding. Very low humidity and strong winds can lead to wildfires in places where the plants are dry or easy to burn. Pollution in the air can cause breathing difficulties, especially for people who have health problems. Extreme temperatures threaten people whose homes lack proper heating or cooling systems.

Blizzard winds can blow over 35 miles (56 kilometers) per hour. Blowing snow makes it hard to see very far.

What's in a Name?

Hurricanes, cyclones, and typhoons are all the same thing: massive, swirling storms that form over warm tropical waters and have winds over 74 miles (119 kilometers) per hour. What people call the storms depends on where in the world they form.

Not only do meteorologists need to predict these conditions, they also need to alert the public to approaching danger. Part of the damage done by Hurricane Sandy happened because the public misunderstood the danger, not because meteorologists didn't expect it.

A weather radio has an alarm that signals dangerous weather approaching.

The National Weather Service can use the Emergency Alert System to warn the public of danger.

Apps can provide severe weather alerts.

Meteorologists communicate to the public through websites, weather apps, and TV weather programs. News stations also pass on weather information.

Officials may close roads when weather makes travel too risky.

When their models predict severe weather in an area based on the current conditions, meteorologists issue a watch. This may be a flood watch, a blizzard watch, or various other kinds of watches. When meteorologists receive reports that the severe weather event is already occurring, they issue a warning. As technology advances and forecasts become more accurate, weather warnings can help save more lives.

A Doppler on Wheels (DOW) truck searches the skies for tornadic activity. At least 1,250 tornadoes occur in the U.S. each year, more than any other country.

Chasing Twisters

Tornadoes are much smaller than thunderstorms. They form suddenly and move rapidly across the landscape. To study them up close, scientists must become mobile. Scientists go where the conditions are right for tornado formation and hope to get lucky. Their trucks carry radar and other weather instruments.

Some communities have loud, outdoor alarms to warn of tornadoes.

CHAPTER SIX

PREDICTING THE FUTURE

Weather models have steadily improved over time. They use increasing amounts of information taken from the atmosphere around the world. Meteorologists have continued to develop their models by studying how real weather events happened in recent history. These improvements are especially important because extreme weather events such as droughts and heat waves are becoming more likely due to global warming.

Oceans have absorbed most of the extra heat added to Earth by global warming.

Temperatures have increased fastest in remote places such as mountaintops.

Global warming may be the cause of droughts that are more frequent and more severe.

Global Warming

Human actions, such as burning fossil fuels, are changing the atmosphere and causing it to absorb more heat. In 2018, the average global temperature was 1.5 degrees Fahrenheit (0.83 degrees Celsius) warmer than average global temperatures from 1951 to 1980. Seventeen of the 18 warmest years measured have occurred since 2001.

Burning fossil fuels puts gases into the atmosphere that absorb extra heat.

Rockets carry satellites into space.

Meteorologists continue to make progress in their ability to predict weather. Powerful new satellites now take frequent, high-quality pictures of the atmosphere.

Some weather satellites circle Earth from the North Pole to the South Pole.

Meteorologists are working to turn the large collection of pictures into a massive amount of data and figuring out how to add this data to their models. They are developing new ways to measure the properties of clouds and understand their role in weather. By studying satellite images soon after they are taken, meteorologists can track storm clouds as storms form.

Weather prediction will never be perfect. No model can include every single factor in every inch of the atmosphere around the world, or every feature of the land. Small errors can throw off the **accuracy** of a model. The further ahead a meteorologist tries to peer, the more these small errors can become large mistakes. Seasonal trends, and trends such as global warming, are easier to predict than weather in a specific place on a specific day.

Still, computer models can sometimes be extremely accurate. When Hurricane Florence approached shore in September 2018, the National Hurricane Center predicted it would land only two miles (3.2 kilometers) away from where it actually did land five days later. The more accurate the prediction, the better people on the ground can prepare, saving both lives and property.

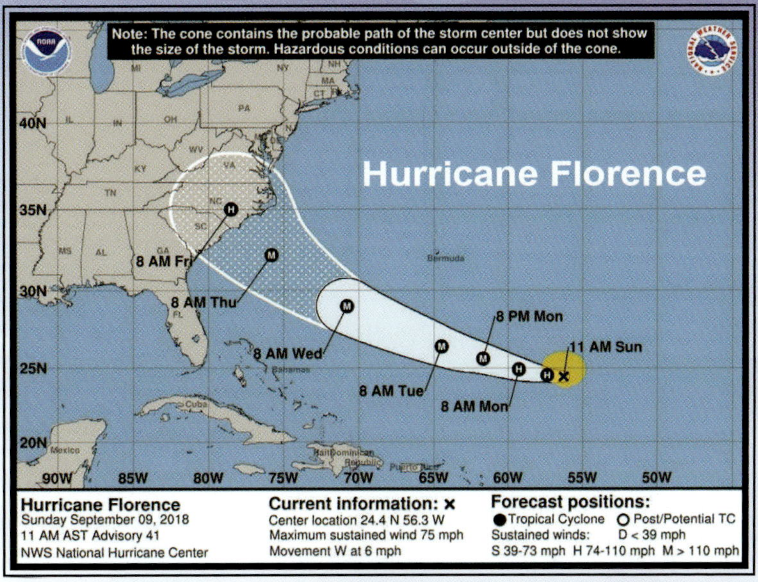

Hurricane Florence made landfall near Wrightsville Beach, North Carolina, on September 14, 2018.

MAKE A BAROMETER

Try predicting the weather yourself by making a simple barometer, a tool that measures air pressure.

Supplies

- ◊ balloon
- ◊ scissors
- ◊ empty glass jar
- ◊ rubber band
- ◊ drinking straw (with no bend)
- ◊ craft glue
- ◊ paper
- ◊ pen or marker
- ◊ tape

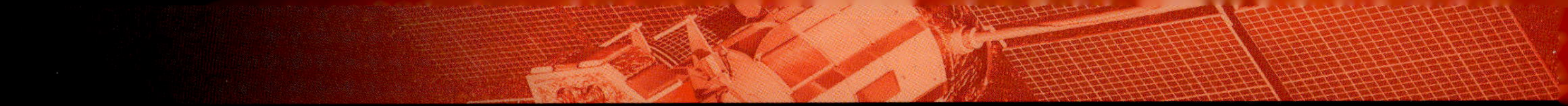

Directions

1. Cut off the neck of the balloon. Stretch the rest tight over the jar opening. Secure the balloon in place with a rubber band.

2. Cut one end of the straw at an angle to make a pointer.

3. Glue the straw across the top of the jar, making sure the uncut end of the straw is in the middle of the balloon.

4. Tape the paper to a wall (check with an adult first).

5. Set the jar next to the paper so that the straw's point crosses over the paper's edge. Draw a line at the place where the point hits.

6. Check the barometer daily. Heavier air will push the balloon down and lift the pointed end of the straw. Make a mark where the straw points. When the straw hits this mark, the air pressure is rising. If the straw point drops down, this means the air pressure is falling. Make a mark for this as well.

7. Rising air pressure often leads to clear and sunny weather. Falling air pressure often leads to precipitation. When your barometer indicates changing air pressure, observe the type of weather that comes your way.

Glossary

accuracy (AK-yur-uh-see): the state of being correct or exact

air pressure (air PRESH-ur): the weight of the air

assumptions (uh-SUHMP-shuhn): things that are assumed to be true or correct

atmosphere (AT-muhs-feer): the gases that surround a planet

humidity (hyoo-MID-i-tee): moisture in the air

latitudes (LAT-i-toods): regions with specific distances north or south of Earth's equator

meteorologists (mee-tee-uh-RAH-luh-jists): people who study Earth's atmosphere

precipitation (pri-sip-i-TAY-shuhn): water falling from the sky to the ground as rain, sleet, snow, or hail

precise (pri-SISE): very exact or correct

probability (prah-buh-BIL-i-tee): how likely something is to happen

satellites (SAT-uh-lites): objects that orbit Earth, another planet, or a moon

sustained (suh-STAYND): constant or continuous

Index

Text-Dependent Questions

1. What is an air mass?
2. What is one method ancient people used to predict the weather?
3. What is a weather model?
4. How do satellites contribute to weather prediction?
5. What is the difference between a tornado watch and a tornado warning?

Extension Activity

Use a notebook or a computer document to record the daily weather. Pick a time such as right after school. Every day at that time, write down the temperature (if you have access to a thermometer—otherwise, note how warm or cold it feels), precipitation, cloud cover, and whether the air feels dry or humid. Do this for several weeks. Do you notice any patterns?

About the Author

Clara MacCarald is a writer with a master's degree in ecology and natural resources. She lives with her family in an off-grid house nestled in the forests of central New York. When not parenting her daughter, she spends her time writing books about science and history for kids.

www.rourkeeducationalmedia.com

PHOTO CREDITS: Cover photos: satelite/hurricane © Andrey Armyagov, Doppler radar © Francois Arseneault, clouds/lightning/ocean © IgorZh; Pages 4-5: Map public domain image courtesy of Cyclonebiskit. Aircraft image, US Dept of Commerce. Page 6-7: shutterstock.com | Inspired By Maps, ©BlueDoorPub, shutterstock.com | Captain Cobi. Page 8-9: shutterstock.com | FashionStock.com, istock.com | seclemens, shutterstock.com | Olga Enger, shutterstock.com | Dmitri Ma. Page 10-11: Editorial credit: / Shutterstock.com, istock.com | Heiko Küverling, istock.com | BrianAJackson, istock.com | NicoElNino. Page 12-13: NOAA, shutterstock.com | Rainer Lesniewski, shutterstock.com | DiKiYaqua. Page 14-15: istock.com | ttsz, shutterstock.com | Vitalii_Mamchuk, NASA. Page 16-17: shutterstock.com | nomad810, shutterstock.com, shutterstock.com | Designua. Page 18-19: shutterstock.com | Vyntage Visuals, istock.com | Nastco, shutterstock.com | Jeff Gammons StormVisuals. Page 20-21: istock.com | DelmasLehman, David R. Ingham- CC BY-SA 3.0, Chris Flook CC BY-SA 4.0 Page 22-23: Telegraph key and sounder Public Domain image by Daderot, shutterstock.com | Edward Haylan, Preussischer Kulturbesitz, Berlin-EDITORIAL. Page 24-25: istock.com | pressureUA, USMil Mil.gov, istock.com | bowie15, istock.com | Vasyl Dolmatov. Page 26-27: shutterstock.com | aapsky and NASA, Shutterstock.com | Artem Zarubin, BDPub, shutterstock.com | Aneese. Page 28-29: shutterstock.com | Rawpixel.com, istock.com | fusaromike, NWS. Page 30-31: National Weather Service, shutterstock.com | Cozy Home. Page 32-33: shutterstock.cOM | Todd Shoemake, shutterstock.com | Dustie, shutterstock.com | Dmitriy Kochergin, shutterstock.com | lavizzara. Page 34-35: istock.com | Images_By_Kenny, shutterstock.com | LesPalenik, shutterstock.com | Andrey_Popov. Page 36-37: istock.com | JANIFEST, shutterstock.com | Eddie J. Rodriquez, 61625734 Eldar Nurkovic | Dreamstime.com, shutterstock.com | StarLine, istock.com | tobynabors. Page 38-39: shutterstock.com | Carmen Avram, shutterstock.com | Mavrick, istock.com | quintanilla. Page 40-41: NASA/National Weather Service, istock.com | AdrianHancu, NASA. Page 42-43: istock.com | VK7HIL, istock.com | Petrovich9, NOAA. Page 44-45: shutterstock.com | Colors, timquo

Edited by: Kim Thompson

Produced by Blue Door Education for Rourke Educational Media. Cover and interior design by: Jennifer Dydyk

Library of Congress PCN Data

Weather Prediction / Clara MacCarald
(Science Masters)
ISBN 978-1-73161-465-0 (hard cover)
ISBN 978-1-73161-272-4 (soft cover)
ISBN 978-1-73161-570-1 (e-Book)
ISBN 978-1-73161-675-3 (e-Pub)
Library of Congress Control Number: 2019932382

Rourke Educational Media
Printed in the United States of America,
North Mankato, Minnesota